Silence
God Loves You So

Ruby Dell Ross

authorHOUSE®

AuthorHouse™
1663 Liberty Drive
Bloomington, IN 47403
www.authorhouse.com
Phone: 1-800-839-8640

© 2009 Ruby Dell Ross. All rights reserved.

No part of this book may be reproduced, stored in a retrieval system, or transmitted by any means without the written permission of the author.

First published by AuthorHouse 7/17/2009

ISBN: 978-1-4389-5692-3 (sc)
ISBN: 978-1-4389-5693-0 (hc)

Library of Congress Control Number: 2009903040

Printed in the United States of America
Bloomington, Indiana

This book is printed on acid-free paper.

Dedication

This book is dedicated to:

Alma Kearney
Ollie Fitzhugh
Thelma Mathews
Daniel Matthews
Max

Contents

Tribute To "Our Father"	1
Majestic	2
The Wind	3
In His Love	4
An Observation	5
Somebody	6
What's Tomorrow For	7
Spring Excerpt	9
The Earth Is A Battlefield	10
What A Beautiful World	11
God Reigns Eternally	12
Just Over The Horizon	13
Silence	15
Only Thee	16
Wast Thee	17
My God Abideth	18
Christ Alone	19
Christ Will Come	20
Christ Reigns	21
Growth And Development	22
Feats and Patience and Love	23
Further Along	24
Master! O Master!	25
Always In Christ	26
This Great Sailor	28

I Look To My Saviour	29
Craftsmen Unkind	30
Blue Jeans	31
What You Talking	34
Insensitive Clods	35
I'm Gonna Pray	36
Wisdom's Child	37
My Sacred Holy Friend	38
Rotunda	39
My Most Fortunate Find	41
I Thank My God	42
According To His Word	44
Be Quiet My Spirit	45
Keeping The Faith	46
Pastime	47
The Fact Is	48
True Confession	49
The Promised Land	50
The End Result	51
Today	52
Living To Live	53
His Love	54
Daily Living	55
Sweet Savior	56
No Need To Linger	57
Live On, Live Long	58
Christmas	59

Christ	60
God's Infallible Gift	62
Pursuit of Happiness	64
Charter Your Way	65
I Just Know That	68
I Am	71
A Lock On a Door	73
A Friend	74
Crown Jewel	75
To Love Him	76
Forever	78
The Hills Getting High	79
Praise And Adoration	80
I Ask, Dear Lord	81
To Thee I Pray	82
In Heaven	84
Prayer	85
I Truly Uphold	86
Daily Prayer	87
I Pray	89
I Beg Of Thee	90
Dear Jesus	92
Imploration And Gratitude	93
Submission	94
I Am But A Sinner	95
Dear Father In Heaven	96
Thank You Jesus	97

God Loves You So	98
Invitation	99
If	100
O Wanton Soul	101
I Am Persuaded	102
O Soul Of Mine	103
So Glad I Got The Chance	104
Jesus! Jesus! Jesus!	105
Seek Ye First The Kingdom of Heaven	106
The Extension of Grace	107
Without God	108
Repentance	109
Only Believe	110
Bless Be	111
Daily Regimen	112

Foreword

I am deeply moved by my mother's love for nature and the natural. Her love for her fellowman and her passion for God is beautifully versed in her poetry.

This collection of poetry soothes and acts as a balm to the spirit, soul and mind. God is real and I am convinced that there is healing power in these poems that are full with reflections and testimonies of faith, insight, prayer and praise.

What she gives of herself is grounded in her faith and without a doubt, in her faith there is power.

Pamela A. Ross, MD

Acknowledgements

Taylor N. Ross, "Confessions" original art design.

David L. Robertson, author photograph.

Kirk Perry, ocean photographs.

Thanks

To my daughters Constance, Kimberly and a special thanks to Pamela for making this mission possible.

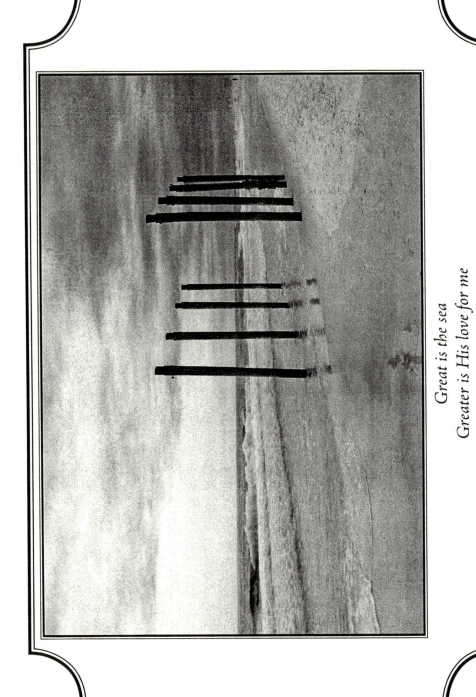

Great is the sea
Greater is His love for me

Tribute To "Our Father"

Our world is flowers and sunshine;

Tears and rain,

Rivers, oceans, streams,

And fresh water springs;

Joys and laughter and dreams,

Plenty yielding fields,

Bounteous crops of grain;

Rich harvests of peace, health and wealth;

Majestic voices to sing

Praises unto His holy name

For all the love He shares,

For His eternal reign.

This is our Father's world.

Majestic

The morning after
A drenching down pour
Dawn's early sun, above a hue of varied clouds,
Plays hide and seek.
Trees sway gently
While their embryoid buds quest a viewing peek
Of Earth's aesthetic reviving
In fresh garden greens,
In gaily colored petals newly perfumed.

The Earth newly bloomed
'Majestic beauty o'er all the way'
Might only last for the morn
Of one day,
But captured in gracious hearts
Where it forever stay.

Majestic-ness that will never go away;
And, if eyes could talk
They would say:
'majestic beauty o'er all the way;
New birth that's mine
Each and every day.
God's love forever, here
With me to stay.'

The Wind

Uncontrolled as a billowy sea,
Untamed as wilderness beasts;
Harkens never to my plea.

The wind is blustery! Turbulent! Wild!
Possesses the temper
Of a tantrumy child.

The wind howls
A heinous growl
While over the earth
It stalks, and prowls.

Yea! It harkens to the Master,
Then gently it blows
In a voice quiet and low,
Swaying boughs and grasses
In rhythmic sweetness to and fro.

In its tranquil temperament,
Or in its hostile imprisonment,
The Peace comforts and solaces me.

In His Love

I am a shallow
        Lacking depth.
I am as busy as a bee
         Though minutely covering the turf,
   The span of the sea.

It's the Good Lord
          That's keeping me;
For, I comprehend little
In His vast domain.

Never a day that stays
The same.
In His love
        I pray to remain.

An Observation

    I look over the fields
And the green grasses on the hills;
Sifting soil through my hands,
Essential substance of man,
Admiring all the good it brings and yields;
Patches of clover, alfalfa, fescue,
Stand tall and green in fields untilled.

    Fresh air that I breathe, fresh water Streams,
Each time I take an observation
I thank God
I am an active part of His Conservation.

    I wonder why so many choose not to
Give God praise?
The birds above nesting in the trees
Just up at once in the sky flying high.
I take a deep breath, I sigh.
I wonder why so many people refuse to
Give God praise?
Man and his rebellious ways…

I view the lakes, ponds, and streams,
Even the erosions and gullies uncovered in green.
The oceans, the seas, the wind and its breeze;
With ease,
I can say, O God, Ruler of the high and low,
Thou art worthy!
Only thee, O God, art worthy to be praised.

Somebody

Somebody walked a winding road.
Somebody carried a much too heavy load.
Somebody ran an endless mile
And never had time to rest, chat, or smile.
Somebody lived affluently,
Very much in style.
Somebody prayed constantly,
"My troubles will be over, O Lord, after while."

The life you live you can't ignore.
Whose life you live you will never know.
Be assured,
It's been lived before.

Was it yours, or the neighbor next door?
Was it that drunkard
Passed out on the barroom floor?
Was it the big time drug dealer?
Was it the abused child
Prominent society saw fit to defile?
Was it the prowling thief, the insidious cheat,
The master of lies?

Be it ever so wise,
Walk always as straight as you can.
You may come to live your life
Over and over again.

Life with its intricate patterns never change,
But God will rearrange any repentant change
To make a sinful life nevermore the same.

What's Tomorrow For

What's tomorrow for?
    For little miracles
        To happen.

What's tomorrow for?
To reconstruct the today
That was yesterday;
   To make a better way;
To hurdle us over those hurdles
Unknown, unseen,
   Undreamed,
      That within our paths
        Secretly lay.

What's tomorrow for?
To rid malice
That upon innocence stalk and prey;
To watch and wait,
    And pray
      For the coming
Of a new world
Full with godly divisions
Fit for all
To live, to work, to play.

*As a man, his days are as grass:
As a flower of the field, so he flourisheth. Psalms 103:15*

Spring Excerpt

Each new flower
Bathed in heaven sent showers;
A majestic wonder.

Yet I say,
"Never a wonder like me,
Except for the Son
Sanctioned and ordained
By the Holy Trinity."
Spring's message to all:
'Think highly of yourself
Whomever you be.'

The Earth Is A Battlefield

The Earth is a battlefield
Full with vestured soldiers
Marching as to war;
Stationed on every post,
On every terrain and coast,
From seashore to seashore,
And with the Holy Word equipped
As we live out our soldiership.

The Earth is a battlefield
Where all brave men live.
Sergeants of truth, of trust,
Of faith.
Warriors furloughing in hope,
In patience, in love, in grace;
Enlisted persons of every race.

Women and children, too, are
Vestured soldiers
Marching as to war.
Christ Jesus our Comrade,
Our Colonel;
The General who leads us
Through every conflict on until
The battle we win
As we become conquerors over sin.
Though our victory already won
When death was vanquished
By the Risen Son.

What A Beautiful World

Beautiful water,
        Peaceful river,
    Meadows shady, grassy, and green,
      All resting beneath a hardy hike
        Below a towering hillside.

This picturesque scene
     Induces one's mind to take the body
      And lull, and relax, and dream,
        Somewhere mid mingled scents
      Of Spring's fragrant blooms.

Beautiful water,
      Peaceful river, tranquil stream;
Barefoot in cold mountain water
Where brisk chills wake me
      To a shivery summer mood.

My eyes gleam succulence
While trudging upward and o'er
A sub vertical hillside to
        The mountain top.

      From there,
   I view my world in solitude,
  An intangible that yields peace
      To my soul;
    Strengthens greatly
My spiritual self.

God Reigns Eternally

I look over the earth
And gather all I see:
Forest and fields,
Pastures and hillsides,
Grounds freshly tilled.
New leaves on the boughs
Sway quietly in a silent breeze.

I look over the earth
And gather all I see:
Grass in new coats of green,
Lakes and mountains,
Ponds and streams.
Spring lets me know
God reigns eternally
And Supreme.

Just Over The Horizon

Just over the horizon
Another sandy beach,
Another sea shore,
Or
More land beyond our reach.

Just over the horizon
Right where the sun sets
Another vastness of water,
Stream, or rivulet.
Why seek the horizon and beyond
When beneath our feet
There is work that ought be done?

Just over the horizon
Another shoreline,
Another unnourished mind.
Why yet do we boast
Another gold mine?

Just over the horizon
Another seashore
To be washed away
Before morn, before day.
Why choose to disobey?
Is it not the mind of children to long
Their selfish way?
Didn't Judas find it worthless
To deceive, to betray?

Just over the horizon
Another mountain range,
Another time change;
And, the horizon just begins
Where Earth and sky blends.

Just over the horizon
The fog drifts low.
Fog,
A state of confusion you know.

Were men on Earth
A little bit proud
Sodom's sins would be disavowed.
Why seek the horizon and beyond
When our soul's salvation
We simply neglect;
And some things that damns
We give our all to protect?

Just over the horizon
Where the moon greets the sea;
Where the Earth welcomes waves;
Where love beckons me;
Where the ocean blue transcends to the sky…

There above that watchful eye.
There above
Everlasting love.

Silence

    The whisper is as quiet as
The snow that's falling;
As hushed as the Savior
That's ceaselessly calling,
He who bids me come!
            Live forever! happy and free
                In the land
                  Of Eternity.

    As noiseless as the cold
That chills the air;
He bids me climb
The heavenly stair,
            Renew my soul,
            Keep on keeping on
            In the Good Shepherd's fold.

    As still as the frost
That lay over the ground
He covers me
Without a sound,
And promised
            Always to be around.
            No greater friend
            Can be found.

Only Thee

All power cometh from thee,
    Lord;
        Only thee,
            Only thee.

Who can keep my enemy
From a successful conquest?
Only thee, Lord;
Only thee.

Who show the birds
To build a nest?
Who navigate their course
        From East to West?
            Only thee, Lord;
              Only thee.

    Against tempest storms
    When I am tossed about,
Bowed, swayed and bent,
Who can keep me from harm?
Who can let me stand?
    Who can hold me up
        Even on sinking sand?
            Only thee, Lord,
            Only thee.

Who has all things at his command,
And all power in his hands?
        Only thee, Lord,
           Only thee.

Wast Thee

Wast thee, O Lord,
Who kept me
From conception to cradle,
From cradle to bed,
On until I could decipher
My feet from my head;
On until now,
Yet in thy blessed school
Of learning,
   Sorting and discerning;
And again learning
And understanding
      And knowing the worth of thee,
Of knowing and realizing
The greatest love for me;
Of the worth of serenity to
Thine only son,
Whom, like thee,
First loveth me.

Wast thee, O Lord,
Who kept me
From conception to cradle,
      And thee keepeth me yet.

My God Abideth

I will never be able to show you
His footsteps.
I will never be able to show you
His shadow.
But, He abideth. My God abideth.

Christ Alone

O Lord! By your works alone,
I am saved.
No longer to sin
Am I enslaved.
Though my prayers to thee,
I must entreat
To cast away evils,
My soul's defeat.
Christ alone is all I own
He who died,
My sins to atone.
Christ! Christ! Christ alone.

Christ Will Come

When to Christ
My life has resigned;
When to Him
I implore, I petition, I pine;
When His Holy Word
Is my striking a gold mine;
When in faith
And patience, I wait
No matter how the foe
May waylay my fate,
Christ will come
In his savored time.

It then is when
The harvest is mine
Plenteous and abundant
As savored as vintage wine,
As savored as eternal time.

Christ Reigns

When I touched the ocean
First time I felt
The rain.
Then I dreamed
Eternal springs
Never running dry.

Thirsty souls
Nevermore thirst.
Turned my eyes,
Lifted my heart to the sky,
Committed my soul.

Surely! Christ reigns
Yonder above the nest
Of an eagle
Far beyond the highest crest.

Growth And Development

Once I saw an ugly man.
Was much more than I could stand,
I dared his hand
To ever touch mine.
That was my ugly mind.
I was blind,
But now I see,
Was positively me
Thrice uglier than he.

Feats and Patience and Love

Sometimes, my life, stormy weather.
Sometimes, it takes days and weeks,
    Sometimes months,
To get myself together.

Once my life was so torn and broken.
To yield to death, I thought I'd rather,
But those boisterous winds silenced
    Their turbulent
        And periling threats,
None life clouds disbursed from the aisles
Of my island and inlet.

Today, with life, I have no qualms;
No regrets.
I learned to weather the storm.

Further Along

        Further along Lord,
Yes, further along.
Every step is yours Lord;
        And, I'm further along.

The world
Is a dirge song,
But with thee Lord,
        My countenance stays strong.

So, Dear Lord,
        I'm further along
With every step
Whether feeble or strong.

I'm trudging onward, Lord,
 Ne'er on my own
        Still, further along.
          Yes, further along.

Keep building my trust Lord,
Where as, still,
        I'm further along.

Master! O Master!

In anger, fierce,
The sea is rolling.
Master! O Master!
I've long set sail
Howling winds
Have tattered the mask,
Mutinous waves
Are pouring in.

Master! O Master!
Alone am I
Without a friend.
Alone am I
Mid wrath of sin.

Master! O Master!
May the sea not be
My journey's end.

Always In Christ

    I have unplanned occasions
Where worry slips in,
Never as a solacing friend.
    While I rebel against
Its invading persuasion, comes then, it seems,
More worry invasions.

    I submit,
Give worry a guided tour;
Giving worry, then,
Reason to be sure
That I in faith cannot endure;
    But always in Christ
My strength rapidly renews.
Always, I remain in His favor

    Oft my courage minutely
Wavers
Cowering minutely a doubting behavior.

    But, always in Christ
My strength rapidly renews.
Always, I remain in his favor.

*Like the waves upon the sea, His love is forever;
His grace and mercy goes on and on and on….*

This Great Sailor

I am a ship from way cross the sea,
Could find no harbor
That would shelter me.
Could find no rest, no prayer, no peace.
Though I sailed all over
The North, the South, the West, the East.
Could find no rock for my
Anchor to hold.
Gave up on my shipwrecked soul.

Then from the Sea of Galilee
This great sailor
Came to me,
Restored this shipwrecked mess,
Ended this wandering quest.

I search no more for sheltering harbors,
Nor rocks for my anchor to hold.
I found myself.
Took charge of my soul.

Was He who deemed me
Worthy to be.
This great Sailor
From the Sea of Galilee.

I Look To My Saviour

When I am sad,
In doubt, in grief, or in despair;
I look to my Saviour
He who surely cares.

When I feel I'm in the devil's snare,
Where I slipped unaware;
When my heart has been broken
In need of repair;
I look to my Saviour
He who heals all wounds;
Is just, is fair.

When I long with someone to share
My triumphs, my victories, my joys,
My tranquil peace serene;
I look to my Saviour,
The Almighty Supreme.

When I think I'm needing a little
Extra love,
When I know I need a little push
Or shove;
Yes! I look to my Savior
In heaven above.

Craftsmen Unkind

Craftsmen unkind
Etched onto my brain
A meddlesome malice
Adding more to my burdens
Making worse
My mental strain.

I already feel life woes
Unbearable_____
None pressures released
When it, the recognition, an omen ill,
Dispatched from the coven.

Were my heart
Not in Christ faithfully cloven,
And my soul unwoven
Within those unbreakable strands
Of His never ending love
Long ago I'd been toppled
By the slightest shove.

Blue Jeans

Blue jeans fade with
   The sunshine;
      Never
         His love divine.
His love is unchanging.
His love never warrants challenge.
   So why the crime
      Treason?
Why, too,
Sacrilegious reason?
   His love is eternal,
     Lasting forever.
        Even when cherished
         Love inclines
To a new love,
His love, still, is there
To cling to.
   His love is as sure
     As clouds are up above.
    His love is as sure
      As the sunshine,
     The wind,
        The rain.
That is why
Faith in Him
Is more than life to gain.
That is why
   His love, none should deny.
    Cause, when all else
      Is gone

His love is all that remains.
His love is as certain
As morning;
    As real
        As stretching, and yawning.
            When death takes you
His love, still,
When new morn awakes you.
It is an everlasting love
Cordial and gentle;
    Welcoming,
        Warm, and understanding.
    Obedience,
His only demanding.
His love is
    Why any yet live.
        So! Why don't you,
            Your heart to Him
                Give?
Then finish your living today;
Tomorrow, live!
    And let live.
        Be content
            And resigned to:
One step at a time,
One day at a time.

    Riches, too oft,
        Buys nothing but pain.
Stock markets soaring!
No profitable gain.
Because, when death takes you,

Left is
    The corpse's remains.
        Indign values
Not worth as an angel's halo.
Why condemn the self
By stealing the glow?
    Will never make the grass
        Grow_____
Just another worthless endeavor
And nothing more.
   To love Him
     Is not a chore.

Indign values for certain:
Deceptions
   That deceive us,
      Judas'
Whom deny us,
Usurpations' daggers
   That slash and divide us,
       Frankenstein's labs
          That strive to defy us.
Blue jeans fade with
The sunshine;
   Never His love divine.

What You Talking

What you talking when you talking
Misconstrued?
What? Your pious attitude
When your shadow over rude?

What you squalling when you living like a hood?
What you living when your living
Ain't no good?

What you preaching
When you preach just as daemon would?
What you walking when you straddling
The fence
When you know it ain't good sense?

Why the judge? What's the jury
When God ain't your defense?

Insensitive Clods

Some folk treat love cruel
Just because they can.
Some folk mistreat love
Because they're
So wrapped in sin.
Some folk are pleasured much
To harass, molest, offend
Especially when they know
You're lone,
Less a friend.
Some folk are insensitive clods
Not reverenced to the Trinity
Belonging to God.

I'm Gonna Pray

There will be tomorrow
Then so, another day.
Catastrophe
Was to Gomorrah.
Catastrophe
Was to Pompeii.
Kentucky had a new
Waterway.

Same could happen, catastrophe
To Coven's Town,
Tallahassee, or Bombay.

There will be tomorrow.
Then so, another day.
But, today,
I'm gonna pray.
Then, no matter the catastrophe
I can take flight from tomorrow
Into a brand new day.

Wisdom's Child

The Cornerstone rejected.
Still, with heaven's shield of love undying,
The Cornerstone eternally protected.

So, I believe,
Ne'er a man more fortunate
Than "I";
Though he's sailed
O'er every sea;
And his pockets
Are full with money.
His honeycombs drips
And streams with honey.

The fortunate man has supped from every
Vintage wine;
And with kings he freely mingles
And dines.
His clothing nothing but fine!
Tailored and fashioned,
Elite design.

He may even possess the most
Intellectual mind;
Maybe, somewhat,
In touch with divine.

He has lived in castles
That tower toward the sky.
Ne'er a man more fortunate
Than "I".

My Sacred Holy Friend

Once I am shred through injustice,
The port of evil men
Whose abominable ships are driven
To sail pure oceans
And pollute them with sin.

I, solely, in dire need of redemption
And repair
When trampled o'er by
Vile creatures unfair.

Once I am shred through injustice,
The port of evil men
Whose hearts are hardened with rods of steel,
Villainous creatures; notorious!
Having no will to eternally live;
Immoral fools creating nothing but
Oceans of detriment and despair.

Once I am shred through injustice,
The port of evil men,
I o'er sin could ne'er win
Were it not for Christ Jesus,
My sacred holy friend.

Rotunda

Yesterday has passed
And gone;
Far from home and all alone.

I traveled distances far
Searching for a star.
Crossed many rivers I thought were seas,
Stayed oft upon my knees
Asking God to lead me please.

I followed his way.
That's why I am safe and home
To stay.

This world I am in
Is not for tyrants play.
This world I am in is not for those
Who lust high pay.

This world I am in is for those
Who traveled distances far
Searching for a star;
Though yesterday has passed
And gone,
Far from home
And all alone;
But never tossed by tempest storms
And hostile winds.
Weakened sails are nevermore blown.

My heart, ache and pain, nevermore.
My peace, nevermore rented and torn.
My mind, nevermore fogged in densities
Of stress and strain.
No man maketh me ashame,
Though oft my soul caught up
Mid his vile game.

I remember my name.
Materially, I profited none.
My soul, I retain,
And my priceless treasure remains.

What doth it profit a man
To gain the whole world
And lose his own soul?
On Heaven's scroll,
My name, eternally enrolled.

Yes, I traveled distances far
Searching for a star.
I found myself.
I know who I am, and from whence
My every breath.
I came to know Jesus
The Eternal Star,
The master and savior
Who borne me into eternity.

My Most Fortunate Find

Thee came to show the path to go
Thee came to me.
I didn't know.

      I opened not for thee
      A cordial door.
      Yet still, my soul,
      Thee did not ignore.
      Supplied me with all I needed
      And even more;
      And, I never once to heaven
      Did obeisance, pine or implore.

Thy goodness, I thought,
An awful kink within thy mind.
I never thought: love pure and holy,
Love divine.
      I never knew one's heart
      Was so designed
      To give of one's self to a life
      So unpleasant, so unkind.

Thee tarried so patiently with me
Reshaped, rearranged my mind.
I'm nevermore a creature
      Zealously blind.
      I live nevermore to dishonor
      That that's divine
      And thee, my friend,
      My most fortunate find.

I Thank My God

I'm gracefully aging,
Though not forgetting
I'm wonderfully blessed;
And, I pray,
My conquering o'er Satan
An infinite success.

In spite of foul play
By those who plunder, harass,
And molest,
I'm gracefully aging.
Wishing for one hundred and three.
I'm wishing, too,
For tens of thousands
And ninety-three.
I'm wishing for life everlasting,
An infinite eternity.

In spite of obstacles
And dismay
I'm aging within His holy word
Each and every day.

I thank my God
For His spirit of truth
Raptured and forever free.
I thank my God
For this youthful spirit
That he allows to dwell in me.

I am gracefully aging
Wishing for one hundred three,
Wishing, too,
For tens of thousands
And ninety-three.
I am wishing for life everlasting,
An infinite eternity.

I thank my God
For His spirit of integrity.
I thank my God
For His Holy Spirit
Abiding within the heart of me.

According To His Word

God sent
His only son
To direct my path to go.

If I should miss a turn
And find myself
On an unchartered route,
My soul,
He won't forget about.

He'll never say
"I told you so."
He'll take my hand
And direct my path to go.

Be Quiet My Spirit

Be quiet my spirit.
Be hushed in my silence.
Let my mind be stilled.

While on my knees
In solemn prayer
                Requesting from Heaven
                  God's love and care,
                    It, my mind,
Roam free
And wander to crowded places
Instead of to
Pious spaces.
                    Where therein,
                    I see many faces
                  And hear voices still.

Be quiet my spirit.
Be hushed in my silence.
Let my mind be stilled.

Keeping The Faith

I will place the shadow behind me,
The light over and ahead of me,
The path in front of me;
I will keep heaven's faith
Inside of me.

I'll continue in hope, in trust,
To upward press on;
Gather courage and strength from every storm;
Never fearing none that can do
My body harm.

Never will I walk alone,
Even while lone
And on my own.

Pastime

When the labor
   Is but joy
      When toils are not
         A chore
Then to reap is but a pleasure
And the learning
   Is but a treasure
      The crop
         An endless measure
            Whether the gleaming
              Feed the world
Whether the gleaming
Feed one mouth

The Fact Is

This world thrives
On crippling and maiming
Innocent hearts.

This world thrives
On witchcrafts, voodoo,
Computer smarts,
And satanic arts.

Nevertheless,
I thrive, and yet survive
Through, by, and on
The power of God.

True Confession

I may never
My story told;
But, I never sought to destroy
A man's soul.

I may never
My story told;
But, heaven has always
Been my goal.

I may never
My story told;
But, Christ is savior
Of my soul.

The Promised Land

    I was born in the promised land
Where the horn of plenty
Was reaped
By the sweat upon Grand Pa's brow.
    I stopped oft to pray,
Thanking God for the bountiful harvest
That a scale could not weigh.

    I was borne in the Promised land
Where the horn of plenty
Was reaped
By the labor of Grand Pa's hands.
    The harvest is plentiful,
Though the cost is up.
Still, from the silver cup,
I freely sup.
Could be taken away
Anytime, any day.

    I stop oft to pray
Thanking God for the abundance
He sends each day.

The End Result

It never pays
When one believes
Never to pray.

It never pays
When one believes
Never to obey.

It never pays
When one believes to prey
Upon innocent lambs
And trusting pillars.

Wherefrom
The struggling boughs,
The weeping willows.

Today

Satan!
You spend your time seeking:
To control my soul,
To overthrow my mother country,
To deny my God,
To annihilate my existence.

Satan!
I'll talk to you big and bold.
Today is my today,
My never- ending time.
No today of mine
Will be counted as nonprofit,
And never as wasted years.

God gave me victory eternally
Through faith in Jesus;
In blood, in sweat, in tears.

Living To Live

I am living to live.
To Christ, my life,
I must freely give;
Then my service to humanity
Is freely and justly yield.

Time shall come.
This body will die.
I shall live again
As truth testify.
My soul shall never greet
Nor bow beneath Satan's defeat.
My soul shall never meet
The judgment fire,
Cause I am living to live
Not living to die.
I am living to live as heaven
Requires.
I am living to live
My soul's desire.

His Love

Deeper into me
And closer to Him
Is where His love led me.

Away from me
And wholly to Him
Is where His love led me.

To a place where every
Soul should strive to be,
Heavenward,
Is where His love led me.

Daily Living

Coming in, and riding to…
Coming in, and riding through
Daily storms
That may or may not hinder you.

Nevertheless,
Leave never the mind
To unearned stress.

Send upward a prayer.
Give to the Savior His just regard.
He'll keep you in His love and care.

Sweet Savior

Love, forever
To cherish and uphold
The Savior sweet
Whom salvage the soul.

Fear thou never
Of growing old.
Fear thou never
When the body waxes cold.
Savior divine,
Sweet Savior saves the soul.

No Need To Linger

Back and forth
Through the hands of sin
Went the soul of man.
Then the Lamb was slain.
So through the hands of sin
Man has no need to linger
He has a Saviour.
He has a friend.

Live On, Live Long

Live on, live long,
My short lived memory.
Live on, live long,
Survive forever.

Live on, live long,
My storehouse and treasury,
Not mine ever
To call my own.
Just mine temporary,
An entity on loan.

Live on, live long,
My short lived memory.
Live long, live on,
Throughout all eternities.
Live forever, my soul.

Christmas

The mind of the matter:
Eat until you are stuffed,
Eat, even though you've had
More than enough.

The heart of the matter:
Friends, gifts, cheer, and chatter;
A big roasted turkey
With trimmings on a platter.

The soul of the matter:
Thinking more than twice, or thrice;
Giving thanks to God
For the Born and Risen Christ.

Christ

It doesn't matter when
Christ was born,
But why not celebrate
On Christmas morn?

We celebrate our birth
We of nil worth.
Now who are we?
Rogues, less than angels,
A sinful pedigree.

We celebrate our birth
Each and every year.
We esteem this day
With gifts, and noise, and cheer.

It doesn't matter when
Christ was born,
But why not celebrate
On Christmas morn?

Christ was born
To set men free.
Let us be thankful
That He,
Among us, did live
To teach us how to love,
To live, and forgive.

It doesn't matter when
Christ was born,
But why not celebrate
On Christmas morn?

Let us bow
On bended knee
Thanking Him for His grace, His mercy,
His love beyond degree.

God's Infallible Gift

The holiest child
 Sacred and divine,
God's infallible gift
 To all mankind.
Yes! God's infallible gift
 Blameless from life
And free from crime.

Baby Jesus, God's infallible gift,
 The beginning of
An infinite king.
 The commencing of
An Omnipotent Plan
 So wayward man
Might live again.

God's infallible gift,
 The Holy Christ Child,
Was sent to save us from sin
 So over death's victory,
We, too, can win.

God's infallible gift,
  Our Saviour, our friend.
After death we too, like Him,
  Can ascend.

Consider the lillies of the field, how they grow; they toil not, neither do they spin. Matthew 6:28

Pursuit of Happiness

Will my flowers again, in April,
Be covered with snow?
My flowers aren't all jonquils,
And crocuses, you know?

Will my rose bush sprout and bud
Profusely, and green,
Then produce no blooms
For the month of June?

Will I, again, cultivate my garden soil,
Plant new seed,
Watch them sprout, watch them grow,
Watch them spoil?

Labor is work. Labor is love.
Love is toil.

Will my most desirous moods
Become unproductive and fading thoughts?
Will I spend too much time sitting
Around to mope
Not giving thought to my garden as I ought.
Will I give up hope?

Love is cultivating the soil.
Labor is work. Love is play.
Labor is love. Love is toil.
Love renders time to pray.

Charter Your Way

     Life is all about summits, pinnacles,
Points, and peaks,
One whole world absolute and complete.

     Life is about sand castles and paper astrodomes
To be washed away come the first rain storm.
Life is about eternal breathing, inescapable death,
Sinking mud holes.
And the Conqueror who came to save lost souls.

     Life is about cowardice, bravery, and fears,
Uphill tugs and downhill spills;
Finding the right road and steering it clear
Of bumps, dents, crevices, and havocking frills.

     Life is a door open, shut, and closed,
Keeps no man out, locks no man in.
Life is no game of demon play,
Nor vengeance on evil friends.

     Be the brave explorer
And see how many worlds you can discover,
How many friends you can win,
And become the starship captain in a miniature universe
Where life has no end.

Let the summits, pinnacles, points, and peaks,
Be your minor conquest.
Allow human life to be what you love best.
Build no sand castles nor paper astrodomes.

Build on marble, steel, rock, and stone.
Make an escape from death,
Then charter your way through world's unknown
By taking the Eternal Breath.

For the earth shall be full of knowledge of the Lord, as waters cover the sea. Isaiah 11:9

I Just Know That

I just know that
Boy meet girl,
Then fall in love,
Then vow with
Blessings from above;
Forever, in
The name of love.

I just know that,
That's all I know.
If two are
To become as one.

For any other way
I'd be unfree,
And the struggle for truth
And the fight for freedom
Could never be won.

And, so,
That is why that
True love must be
For to enslave no souls,
For to set
Faithful hearts free.

I just know that,
That's all I know;
If two are
To become as one;

Boy meet girl
Then fall in love,
Then vow with
Blessings from above;
Forever,
In the name of love

I'm not saying that
That exist nothing more.
The possibility of?
I think not
A leeway of chance.

I just know that
True love must be.
Long, and lone
I've been in bondage chains,
In tears, in grief,
In pain,
Rented by morals owning
No shame.
Exist no friend to claim.

My inmost
And vast domain
Became a bartered door.
No trusting guard
To ward the enemy.
No true love
To abort the foe.

And, so,
My spirit heaped in woe.
No true love
To ward the foe.
No true love
To ward the foe.

Caged in a caldron
Of despair and disgust,
Not soul to rely on.
Just God's word to trust.

That's why I know that
That's all I know;
For to safeguard
The sacred urn,
True love must be.

Boy meet girl,
Then fall in love;
Then vow with blessings
From above.
Forever,
In the name of love.

Any other way
I'd be unfree.
That's why I just know that
True love must be.

I Am

I am a universe
As magnificent as
   The world.

I am a universe;
   A cosmos;
      But, I am just a grown up girl.

I am a country, populated;
   A nation,
      Congregated.

I am a church,
   A building without a steeple.
      Full with
         Unseen people.

I am a body,
An individual,
A person miraculously made.

I am worth more than any amounts of diamonds,
   Silver or gold.
      Mysteriously, I am!
         I am a creature with soul.

I am a child that seek to be
   Pure in heart.
      I am a marvelous
            Work of art.

I am a universe
    Wondrously built.
        A coat of many colors,
            A patchwork quilt.

I am in Christ Jesus,
The man that retrieved us.

I am a universe,
    A being Heaven sent.
        I live by the beat of my heart.
            I am a child of God.

I am somebody!

A Lock On a Door

A lock on a door
    Is useless when broken.
        A lock on a door
Is liken unto a vow
When in love, in faith, in honesty, spoken.
Though when broken
    Yields all leeway
        To every unworthy token.

A Friend

A friend, with you,
    Will walk that extra mile,
        Run that extra lap,
  And
Will be no falseness in his smile.
His heart will be full
With comforting songs.
His arms
  Will be full with LOVE.

Crown Jewel

Love must be the peace
Unshackled.
Love must be the turbulence
Bound.
Love must be the new way
That dying worlds have found.
Love must be those seeds
Scattered o'er fertile ground.
Love must be
The everlasting path we trod.
Love must be
Our undying faith in God.
Love must be the truce
Forever hanging round.
Love must be
Our foundation sound.
Love must be a virgin spring
Forever running free.
Love has got to be the treaty
Between you and me;
Cause,
Love is the crown jewel.

To Love Him

I don't know how
To love Him;
But,
To love Him is all I can.
To love Him is all I can.
To honor all that
His blessedness demands

With His love
I can stand and withstand
Whatever the malice
That may fall upon the land.

To Him I give my heart.
I give my hand,
And honor all
That His blessedness demands.

To love Him is all I can.
To love Him is all I can.

To Him I'll be truthful and loyal.
What's more royal
Than true love
In the love of a friend
Forever, and for always?

To love Him is all I can.
To love Him is all I can.

May my voice echo,
Repeat and resound,
Over and over, and over again.
May it sound and never end.

To love Him is all I can
To love Him is all I can,
And honor all
That His blessedness commands.

Forever

Forever is two lovers true
Who to each other
Has vowed, I do.

Forever is two lovers true
Who through
Empyrean mystics
Channel believers through
Unseen impossibilities;
Whence the faith, The Trinity.

Forever can never be
Without Him
Who is Everlasting,
Who is Infinity.

The Hills Getting High

The hills getting high,
The knolls getting steep.
But I,
   A charge I have to keep,
Though it oft dwindle me sad,
And oft I weep.
   Don't got much longer
This road to trod.
When I make this journey
My thanks to God.

Praise And Adoration

Father of all seasons,
Times, and reasons;
Father who redeem men from graves
Of treacherous treason;
Father of unknown legions,
Who abide and rule over all celestial
And terrestrial regions.

Father of unity,
Father, my creator, the restorer of me;
Father to whom my prayers
I entreat;
Father of my faith, my hope,
My trust; my reliance.
May I forever live beneath
Your sacred compliance.

You are the greatest in my life,
The grandest in my eyes.
You are the power with all the might,
The Spirit eternally wise.

You are the arm with all the strength,
The heart with all the love;
The giver of knowledge and love immense.
Thanks for standing
In my defense.

I Ask, Dear Lord

    Father in heaven,
Please bestow upon me the will
To wholly obey,
And to walk with thee
All the way
Each and every day.

    Too, oft, I fear, it seems,
That I'm about my selfish way.
Often time
Fear is the power that sways,
And uncomfortable past experiences
Has too,
Its powerful power play.

    I ask, Dear Lord,
Let not present fears
Nor past experiences become
Those stumbling blocks in my way.

    I ask, Dear Lord,
Please falter and fail my enemies,
Those nations who are about life's
Chaos, obstruction, and dismay.

To Thee I Pray

    Fault in my walk,
Fault in my talk,
Unkindness in my thoughts
Thee may find every day
    Forgive me, o Lord,
And strengthen me, I pray.

    So often
I choose not the right words
To say.
Oftentimes
    I take an atrocious path
When I know a better way.

    Inadvertently
Of those many errors I make
I haven't a clue.
That's why I seek forgiveness
And yield my life to thee.
I desire a better me.

    So between me and thee
I wish for an open line.
I seek
To keep an open mind.

    To thee I petition. I implore. I pine.
It is thee who takes away my sins.
It is thee who causes a rift
To mend.

   It is thee whom is
Forever my friend.
It is thee who demands
No vendetta to pay.
It is thee who always knows:
The righteous way;
The wretched heart;
The rebelling soul;
Those sheep who wander astray.

   O Lord, my God,
The Omnipotent One,
To thee, I pray
Many times and oftentimes
Throughout each livelong day.

In Heaven

Keep me focused on thee,
O Lord,
All the day long.

Keep my spiritual outlook
On thee
Powerful and strong.
See that I not do
An advertent wrong.
See that I do
No fellowman harm.

When I have lived upon this Earth
My appointed term
May I greet Thee
As I have learned:
In Heaven
Where all souls are free;
In Heaven
Where all souls should strive to be.

Prayer

I want, O Lord,
        Old Satan out of my way.
      He is a beast of deception
      Whose will is to betray.

I want, O Lord,
        Old Satan out of my way.

I want, O Lord,
      A world where children
        Can, in safety,
        Live and play;
    Where children are taught
To love, to honor, to pray, to obey,
And give praise to thee everyday.

I want, O Lord,
        Old Satan out of my way
      Wherever wandering feet
        May stray,
      Wherever one may venture
        To visit or stay.

      This is my prayer,
        O Lord,
And please, make for our world
      A heavenly place
      For a head to lay.

I Truly Uphold

What did I do, O Lord?
Thee my only rescue.
Seem everything I do
         Is wrong,
      And not error of mine
        Never condoned.

Why, O Lord?
It seems my every effort
Is penalized wrong;
Seems my enemy
Is overpowering;
Seems my enemy is, too,
        In wickedness, strong.

I never believed, O lord,
That I could carry on alone.
Never thought I could make
        It on my own.

Please break this antagonizing,
This blighted hold
That's assailing
My struggling soul.

      Thy Omnipotence, O lord,
        I truly uphold.

Daily Prayer

If you aren't ready now
You won't be ready then.
You won't be ready when…
So, live! as God arranged.
Don't make a change.
Don't start acting strange.

Daily prayer
Will keep you in His care.

Pray daily prayers
For deliverance,
And for repentance.
Sisters and brothers
Will intercede
With prayers of intercession
For whatever the transgression.
Sing songs of adoration,
Make this an adaptation.

Daily prayer
Will keep you in His care.

Never sleep on thy anger
No matter the pain that lingers,
No matter the pain that anguishes.

Daily prayer
Will keep you in His care.

Pray that if anything about you
Needs change
God will rearrange.

Daily prayer
Will keep you in His care.

Live your life and live it now!
You'll be ready then.
You'll be ready when
You'll no longer on the earthly stair.

I Pray

    Some wounds are long open
Raw, oozing, smarting;
Like Antarctic glaciers, seemingly,
        Never unthaw,
Like the feast within
The eagle's claw.

    Nevertheless, I pray.
It is writ
Within thy hands the power to heal,
Whatever may be the unkind malady
Please let it be thy will
That my body heals.

I Beg Of Thee

Make me O Lord,
Make me,
Make me thy own.

Mold me O Lord,
Mold me,
Mold me into a vessel fit and strong.

Keep me O Lord,
Keep me,
Keep me in thy protective care.

Let me feel O Lord,
Let me feel,
Let me feel thy presence near.

Like a flower, whoever you are, you're beautiful.

Dear Jesus

You're universal,
A domain incomprehensible, vast!
And I, a mere speck
That you,
Moment by moment, protect.

You're so COLLOSAL,
A giant ever standing tall;
And I, a wee vessel,
Weak, frail, and small.
In my tracks
I often stall.
Sometime I stumble.
Sometime I fall.

That's why on thee
I continuously call:
For your strength to sustain me,
For your love to forever claim me
As an humble servant
In deep contrition bowed.

You bid that I seek thee
Through prayer
To thank thee for
Thy mercy, love, and care.

You grant me the privilege
To call on thy blessed name
For whatever the need
And that you, for me, will intercede.

Imploration And Gratitude

Forgive me Lord
For my bitter tongue.
Thee, I know,
Has all power to strike it numb;
    And, I never more speak one word.
        I never more sing one song.

I thank thee, most Holy Father,
For thy vast understanding.
I thank thee for showing me every
Essence of thy great commanding,
    And why knowledge of thee should
        Be universal understanding.

I thank thee for thy far stretched tolerance,
For thy forbearance.
I am far from reaching par,
Yet you let me see
Into the heart of me,
        All those issues
      That my soul should abhor.

Forever and always,
No matter my span of days,
Throughout every generation, every age
No matter the acts or deeds
I might engage,
    In thy kingdom I'm merely a babe.
    In thy kingdom, forever thy child.

Submission

The Winds Are Summoning And CallinG
The Acorns Are FallinG
For Squirrels To Be A HaulinG
Another Mystery EnthrallinG
And Winter Still A StallinG
The Gust From The Winds Are Cordially LendinG
To Nature's Planned Autumn EndinG
With The Extension Of HANDS CondescendinG

I Am But A Sinner

    I am but a sinner,
A vagrant vagabond.
Help me, Lord Jesus,
To become like thee,
Thou the Blessed Son,
          Thou the Risen One.

    Write on my heart
Thy eternal peace, thy never ending love.
Fill me, O Lord, with thy patience,
With thy mercy, with thy grace;
And clothe my carnal mind
          In thy righteousness.

    Fix my soul,
O Lord, I pray,
To never falter from thy just way,
Whence keeping my soul wholly
From Satan's tyrannous control;
      Thereby, allowing me to stand
        Boldly in the presence
  Of: Our Father, which art in Heaven.

Dear Father In Heaven

Dear Father in Heaven,
He whose reign is infinite;
He whose reign is love;
At whatever task I venture
I ask thee please to give me strength
To carry through
And do as well as I can do
Until my task is done.
And, whatever task
I pursue
May it be pleasing in sight of Thee.

Thank You Jesus

Thank you Jesus
For unnumbered blessings.
Thank you Jesus
For my being in your possession.
Thank you Jesus
For incessant intersessions.
Thank you Jesus
My true confession.

God Loves You So

     Flower blooms left to wither
Are like children on their own
When abandoned and all alone,
When left to meander and roam.
None never knowing they have a Father
Seated on the Great High Throne.
None never knowing they, too, have a Heaven,
An eternal home.

     Flower blooms that's been left to wither
Watch your flowers grow.
Flower blooms left to wither
God loves you so.
Flower blooms left to wither
Just grow and bloom, and bloom and grow,
And wither never ever more.

Invitation

He blesses us
  All through the day.
    All through the night.
      He watches us too,
        We're never out of sight.

  Why don't we invite His love
    Into our thirsting souls?
      We are big empty
        Soup bowls
          Needing to be filled.

We hunger and thirst
  When Christ
    Is not put first.

So come to the Father
  Through His son, Jesus.
    Make of Him
      Your heart's delight.
        He will appease
          A depleted appetite.

If

If you, I have led
To the redemptive hour,
If you have yielded to
    The Omnipotent Power,
If you have enjoyed
    This reading hour
Then my rose will have
    Bloomed,
My jonquils will have flowered.
    If you, I have led
To the redemptive hour
Would indeed be Heaven's blessings
    And my love that poured
The shower;
Whence, swift transition
    In sacredness flower.

O Wanton Soul

O wanton soul
Why not turn away?
O wayward heart
Why not obey?
Why not heed
The righteous way,
And let go the mind to deceive, to betray?

O wanton soul
Why not turn away?
O wayward heart
Why not obey,
And make the world
A fit place to stay?

Let go the darkness
That blights the way;
Enjoy the light
The lamp of day.

I Am Persuaded

I am persuaded by:
      Seasons that change,
      Rhymes, spiritual reasons,
      And phenomenona strange.

I am persuaded by:
      His Holy Word,
  And all the good things I've heard
  About His mercy, His love, His grace.

I am persuaded by:
      The Earth that stands still
    Yet, it and the solar system
      Move at His will.

I am persuaded by:
      The rivers that flow
      And the oceans
  That reach from shore to shore.

I am persuaded by:
      The Holy Scripture
  That tells of His birth, His death,
      His resurrection,
    His heavenly ascension;
      His eternal plan
  And His everlasting protection.

O Soul Of Mine

O soul of mine,
    Central intelligence
Designed by Divine.
Not better can ever be found.
    Old Satan, for a while,
        May have it bound,
Boast about it,
Toast about it
    All about town.
        But, no doubt about it!
Believing soul, committed soul,
Faithful soul,
  Pray about it.
Ain't nothing that God Almighty
Can't unbound.

So Glad I Got The Chance

My sins to heaven,
I have got to tell.
The storm that's raging
Must be quelled.
Got to go.
Got to set a spell
Until the ebbing tide subsides.

Something inside,
It's like I've died.
It is a conscious awakening.
My soul is being tried.
Real tears are being cried.

In His word I fully relied.
In death I never died.
Was a conscious awakening
My sins to heaven…
So glad I got the chance to tell.
My soul is peaceful.
The raging storm
Has quelled.

Jesus! Jesus! Jesus!

    I call on His name
All the time,
    Jesus! Jesus! Jesus!
O gracious Savior of mine;
    O Great Master,
Omnipotent, Divine.
      Jesus! Jesus! Jesus!
O loving shepherd for all mankind

    I call on His name
All the time,
    Jesus! Jesus! Jesus!

He is my bin of trust,
My silo of faith, my barn of hope,
My pasture field of love.

I call on His name
All the time.
Jesus! Jesus! Jesus!
My counselor, my soul's consolation,
My love,
    My flight to eternity.
      Jesus! Jesus! Jesus!

Seek Ye First The Kingdom of Heaven

Of earth and land and water and sea;
Of wind and fire and silver and gold
Man's selfish conquest,
    A lifelong obsessed contest.

Of earth and land and water and sea;
Of wind and fire and silver and gold
Man dreams to conquer o'er all,
    But ne'er the destroyer o'er his soul.

Of earth and land and water and sea;
Of wind and fire and silver and gold;
Man bought, man stole, man sold;
    None saveth man.

Of earth and land and water and sea;
Of wind and fire and silver and gold;
Flowers grow under the sea,
    Ne'er in wind,
      Nor fire, nor silver, nor gold.

Flowers grow on land;
And flowers grow in me.

The Extension of Grace

To save my face,
From heaven came an
Extension of grace.
My sins, myself tried to cover.
Everything I touched,
My sins aimed to smoother.

Myself, my own hands were destroying.
My seeds unfit for sowing.
My crops unfit for reaping.
My soul merely fit
For Satan's keeping.
My tears, all glaciers,
Too cold for weeping.

Then came Jesus,
The true man of fame
And world acclaim.
It was He who pleaded this loathsome
Sinner's case.
It was He who hid my shame,
And my sins He erased.
Love from heaven
And the extension of grace.

Without God

    Without the gift of
Intelligence,
    Without knowledge and wisdom,
Without spiritual vision,
    Without God,
Life would be a water pitcher
Half empty,
Yet nothing to drink.
Nothing would be for a mind's concern.
Ne'er a thought
To drop pebbles in the urn
Death eternal
For a dying fern.

Repentance

From the wind to the earth,
"It was I who set sails on sea."

The Heavens to the earth,
"It was I who let reverie be;
I who articulated earth, wind, fire, and sea;
Set the eternal order, ordained it be."

The sea to the earth,
"It was I, the empty bowl, you filled me."

The earth to the fire,
"It was I whose ills you purged."

The earth to all:
"It is I who sustains for no profit or gain."

After which:
The sinner uttered from sea
Whose voice echoed a dirgeful plea.
"It was I lost in reverie
When fire purged earth whose ills were me.
It is I, still,
Who longs for peace and tranquility.
Have I cried to God to no avail?
Aimlessly, did I drift over seas with imaginary sails?
Should I profit not from truth which doth prevail,
Then it is I who fail?"

Only Believe

Death, the stalking-horse
Between the sinner and the gate,
Stood waiting.
Death in eerie silence, lone, and cold,
Waits to conquer the unsaved soul.

In times like these
A battle is fought
When peace within is being sought.

The sinner's life unfolded.
He witnessed the doom of the sinful man.
Every deed was told
About the man who barter away his soul.

The sinner ebbed to helplessness,
Unable to cope.
Time presented him
With God's blessings and hope.
A cure and an antidote
Against any foe the villain promotes.

The sinner believed.
He steered his ship and veered the fate
That stood between he
And the Master at the gate.

Bless Be

O bless be the soul
That pines the will of God

O bless be the soul
That lives to right a wrong

O bless be the soul
That lifts his praise in song

O bless be the soul
That foretells in a poem

O bless be the soul
That weathers the tempest storm

O bless be the soul
Whose victory is won

Daily Regimen

Gird thyself with the Testaments.
Keep strong and solid
Thy soul's defense.

Know why the Christ was sent;
Love thy neighbor with good intent.

School thyself in the Decalogue;
Keep thy soul safe
From hell's vicious dogs.

Chant often from Psalms a song
Or two;
Take time to quote from Proverbs too.

Peruse thy Bible often, every leaf
Through and through.
Thy inquiring mind will comprehend
Wisdom and knowledge anew.

Submit thyself ceaselessly in contrition
And in prayer,
Your soul's intercession with
The Mediator up there.

Converse with a friend, or with friends;
Share your understanding about
The God of all men.

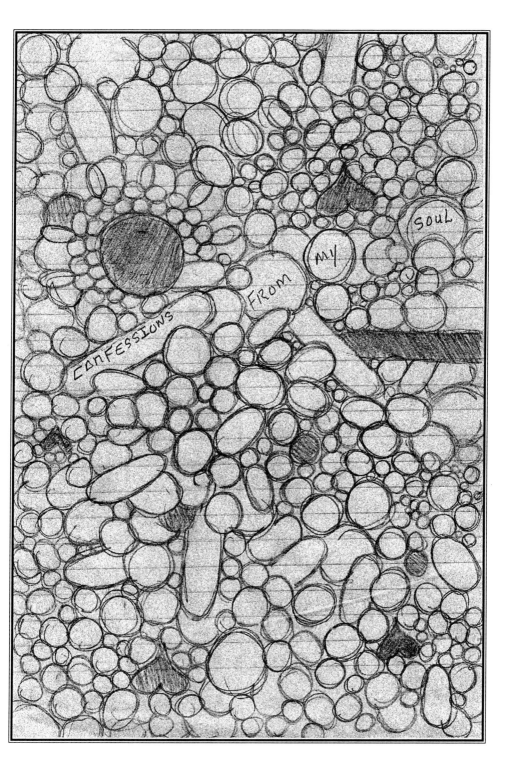

Printed in the United States
154047LV00005B/4/P